I CAN DRAW

I CAN DRAW

DRAW

8 VOLUMES IN 1

GEORGE CARLSON

DERRYDALE BOOKS
New York

This omnibus edition was originally published in separate volumes under the titles: I Can Draw!—Things with Squares, Circles, and Triangles; I Can Draw!—Things I See; I Can Draw!—Figures; I Can Draw!— Cartoons & Funny Pictures; I Can Draw!—Animals; I Can Draw!— Scenes; I Can Draw!—Trees, Flowers, and Fruit; I Can Draw!—and Make a Real Picture. Each individual volume, copyright © The Platt & Munk Co. Inc.

This 1986 edition is published by Derrydale Books, distributed by Crown Publishers, Inc., 225 Park Avenue South, New York, New York 10003.

Manufactured in Hong Kong

Library of Congress Cataloging-in-Publication Data

Carlson, George, 1940–
  I can draw.

  Summary: Provides instructions for drawing figures, cartoons, animals, trees, flowers, objects using squares, circles, and triangles, and other subjects.
    1. Drawing—Technique—Juvenile literature. [1. Drawing—Technique] I. Title.
NC730.C28 1986   741.2′4   86-19817
ISBN 0-517-62540-7

Cover design by June Marie Bennett

h g f e d c b a

CONTENTS

FOREWORD

Welcome to the wonderful world of art. For some, the ability to draw comes naturally; for others, drawing is a creative activity that must be learned, like riding a bicycle. Some develop their ability early in life, while others don't begin until the middle or later years. Some artists choose to follow the lead of their contemporaries, while others prefer the great classic masters. However, all these people have one very important thing in common: each has had to master the basics of drawing.

This edition of *I Can Draw* collects eight separate, original booklets in one volume. It promises hours of fun and enjoyment, while it teaches the rudimentary rules of drawing. From circles, to animals, to cartoons, plus much, much more, budding artists will learn the principles of style, perspective and composition from this thoughtful, well-designed and easy-to-follow book.

Progressing step-by-step, *I Can Draw* provides instruction in eight important areas. The first section, "Things with Squares, Circles and Triangles," explains the use of basic drawing tools and how to construct simple shapes. "Things I See" uses those shapes to build everyday objects, among them a teddy bear, a piggy bank and a rag doll. The third section shows how simple stick figures come to life. The fourth, "Cartoons & Funny Pictures," teaches how to draw faces showing glee, anger and surprise, as well as comic characters.

Section five is "Animals"—easy-to-draw dogs, cats, rabbits, camels, horses, cows and more. Next, the techniques needed to compose "Scenes" are introduced, including simple perspective projection. After section seven, "Trees, Flowers and Fruits," section eight pulls everything together to "Make a Real Picture!"

Drawing is a skill that every person can develop. *I Can Draw* presents the beginner with a straightforward, well-organized guide to the world of drawing. The ability to express oneself is vital; with this imaginative, flexible and practical book the creative process can begin.

D.J. DeChristopher

New York
1986

I CAN DRAW!

Things with SQUARES CIRCLES and TRIANGLES

ok **1**

YOU WILL NEED, ~ FIRST

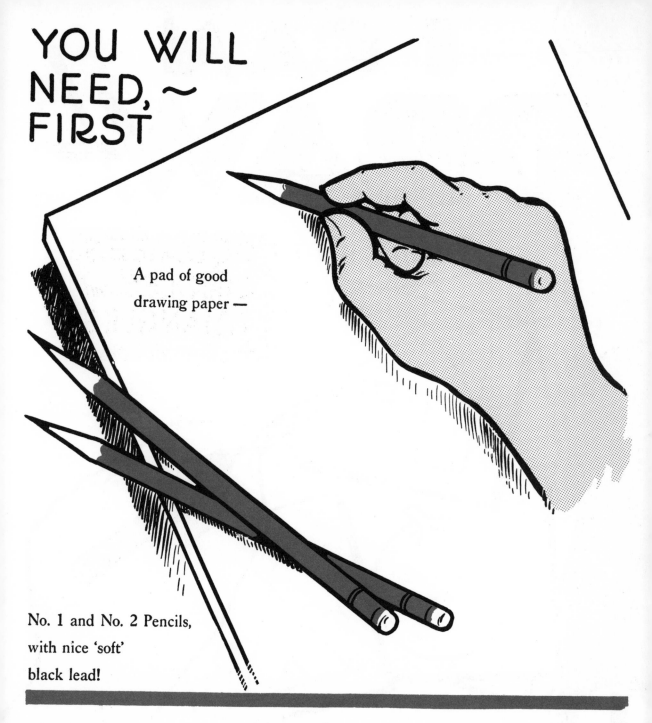

A pad of good
drawing paper —

No. 1 and No. 2 Pencils,
with nice 'soft'
black lead!

and A RULER WHEN YOU DRAW VERY STRAIGHT LINES

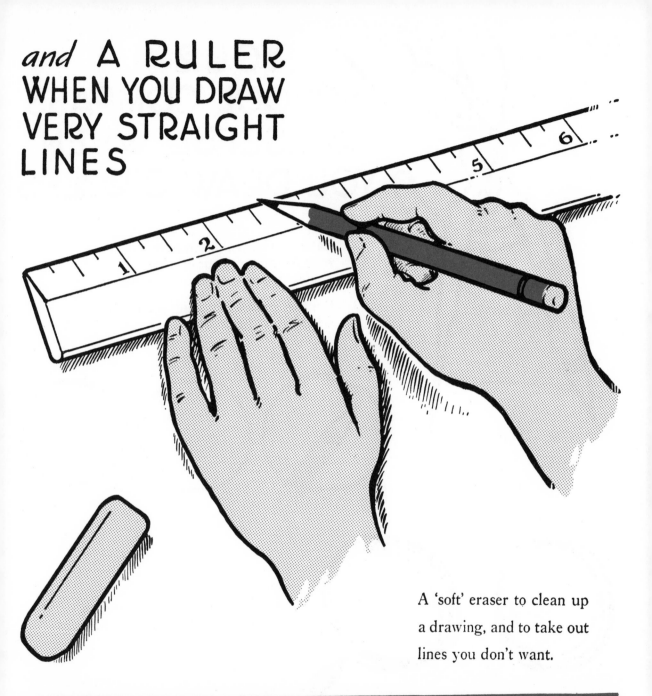

A 'soft' eraser to clean up a drawing, and to take out lines you don't want.

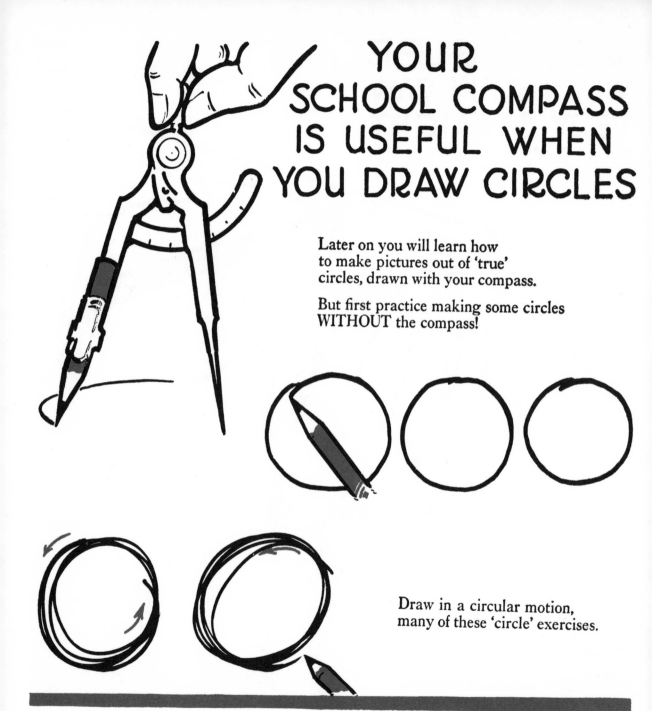

YOUR SCHOOL COMPASS IS USEFUL WHEN YOU DRAW CIRCLES

Later on you will learn how to make pictures out of 'true' circles, drawn with your compass.

But first practice making some circles WITHOUT the compass!

Draw in a circular motion, many of these 'circle' exercises.

and THIS IS GOOD "PRACTICE"

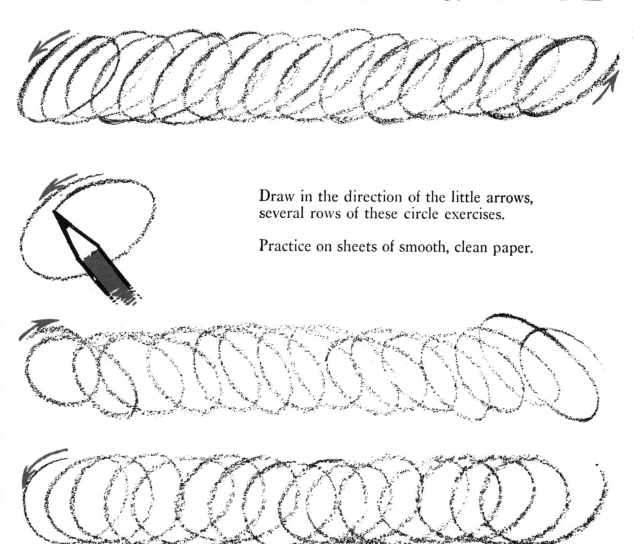

Draw in the direction of the little arrows, several rows of these circle exercises.

Practice on sheets of smooth, clean paper.

MORE LINE "EXERCISES"

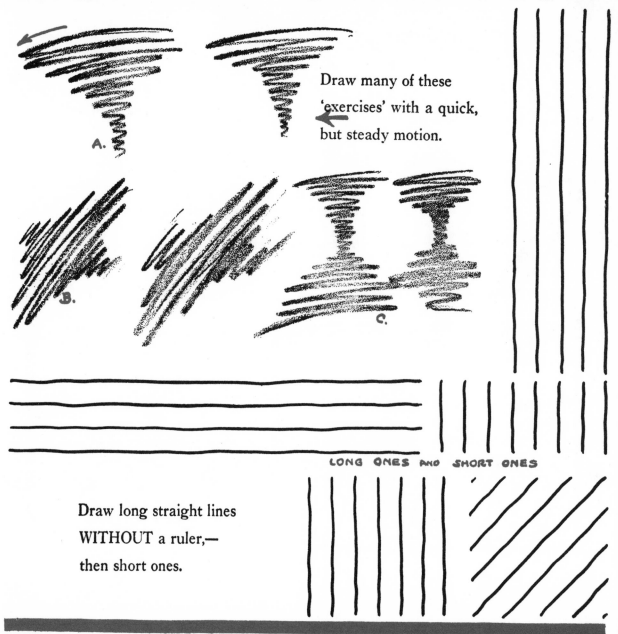

Draw many of these 'exercises' with a quick, but steady motion.

A.

B.

C.

LONG ONES AND SHORT ONES

Draw long straight lines WITHOUT a ruler,— then short ones.

NOW FOR SQUARES ━━━━━━━━ !

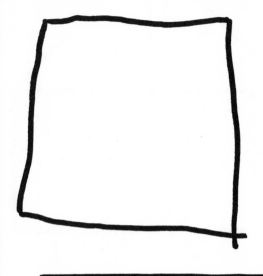

Draw them 'free hand' first,
even if they are not so straight.
It will be good practice.
Then draw them with a ruler.

To find the exact center of a square,
draw light lines as in the square below.
The exact center is point 'A' where
all the lines cross.

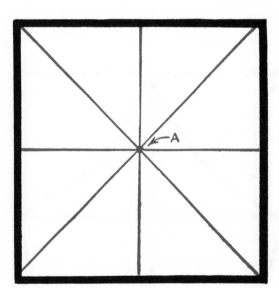

THEN A HOUSE

When you have drawn the square
and the dividing lines, draw
the house as you see it here.

Make use of the cross lines
to find their center points.

Then draw the door and window.

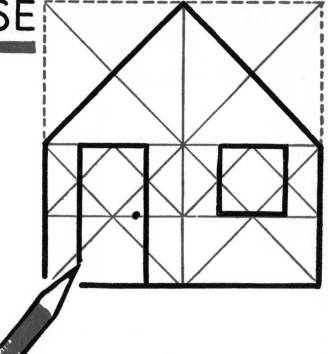

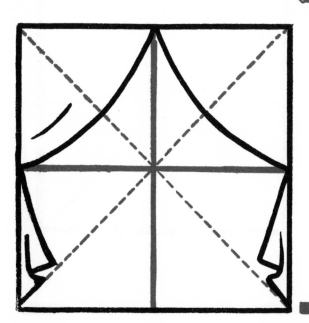

A window is drawn this way.

Find the points where the curtains
begin and end, and then copy them
free hand as shown here.

An APPLE IS EASY!

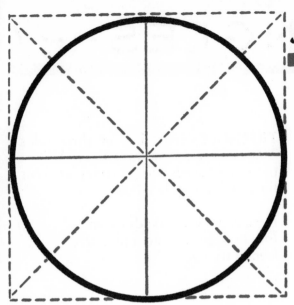

An apple is about the easiest object to draw with a circle.

First draw the circle in a square.
Do it in very light lines.
Then, with a very soft black pencil, draw the circle 'free hand' and put in the stem.

There's the APPLE!

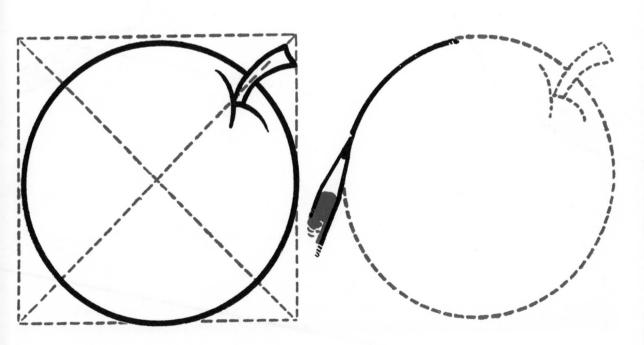

DRAW TRIANGLES····!

TRIANGLES have, lines on three sides. This one is made of three lines, ALL the same length. Some triangles have lines of different lengths.

Here is the way you draw, an Indian wigwam, and a pine tree from a triangle.

MORE THINGS YOU CAN DRAW-

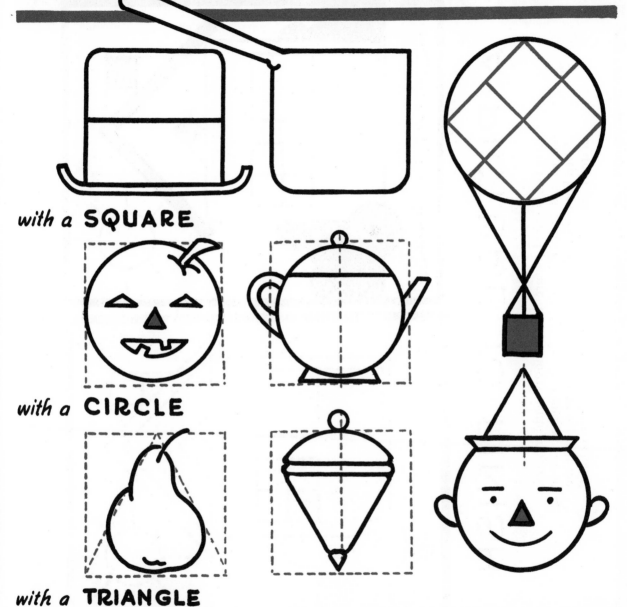

with a **SQUARE**

with a **CIRCLE**

with a **TRIANGLE**

A PICTURE TO FINISH

Here is a finished picture drawn mostly with squares, circles and triangles. Alongside, the same picture in dotted lines. Complete this picture by drawing over the dotted lines with your very black pencil. Then color it!

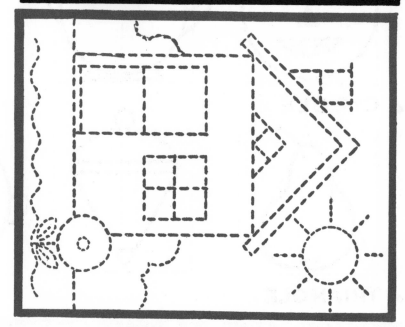

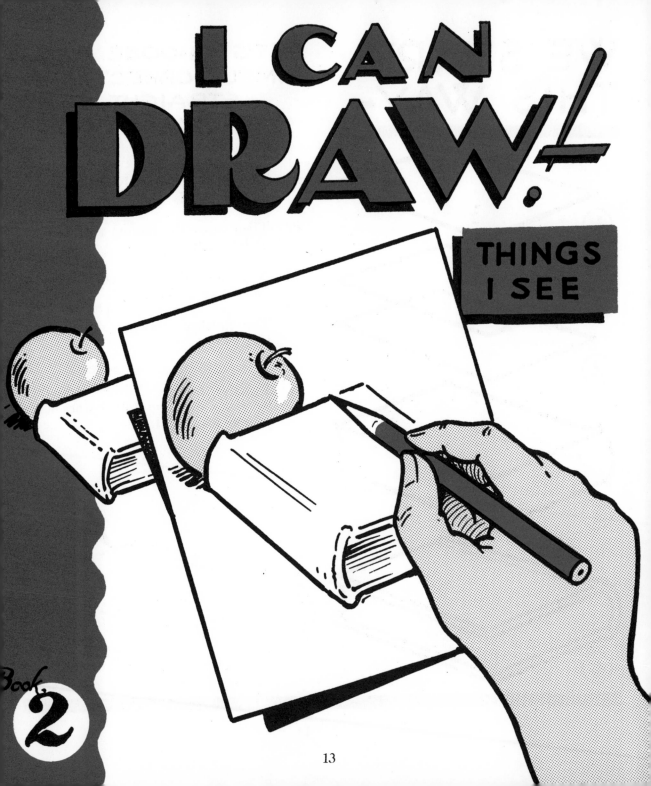

I CAN DRAW!

THINGS I SEE

Book 2

13

WE START THIS WAY~

LET'S CHOOSE A SIMPLE OBJECT IN STRAIGHT LINES ~LIKE A BOOK~

#1—The top of a book, lying flat on a table, is drawn like this,—

#2—Then draw the bottom side exactly under it, this way,—

#3—Now join the three corners so it looks like a book,—

The finished drawing should look like #4.

Practice making finished drawings by going over the dotted lines with your black pencil.

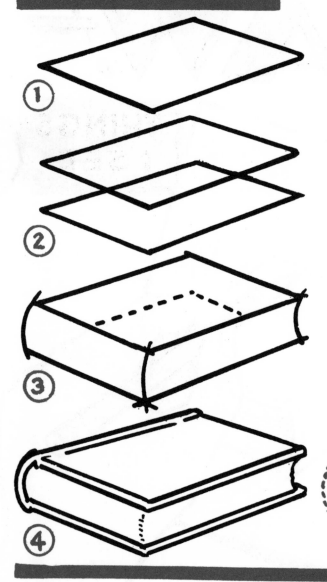

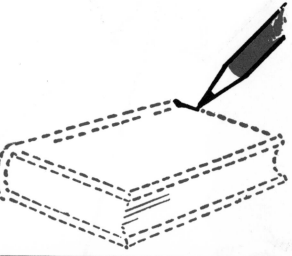

AND-IT IS A PICTURE!

To draw a picture of two apples placed near a book, first draw it in very simple lines (as shown at the top) then finish it as you see here.

Learn to make a finished picture by joining the lines in the dotted diagram.

A "STEP BY STEP" PICTURE

Begin this drawing exactly as you began drawing the book.

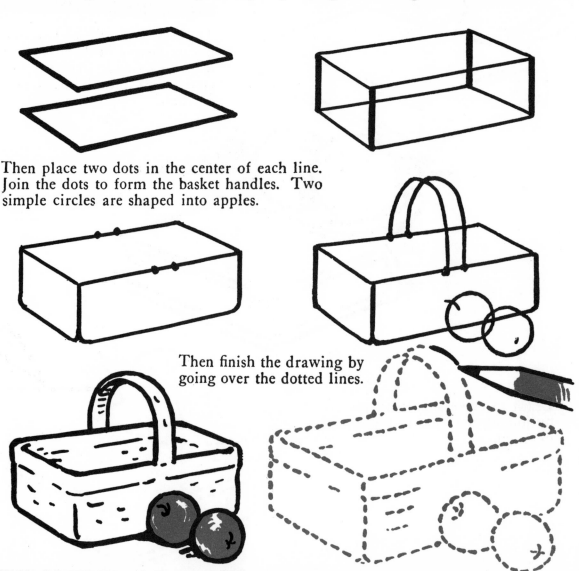

Then place two dots in the center of each line. Join the dots to form the basket handles. Two simple circles are shaped into apples.

Then finish the drawing by going over the dotted lines.

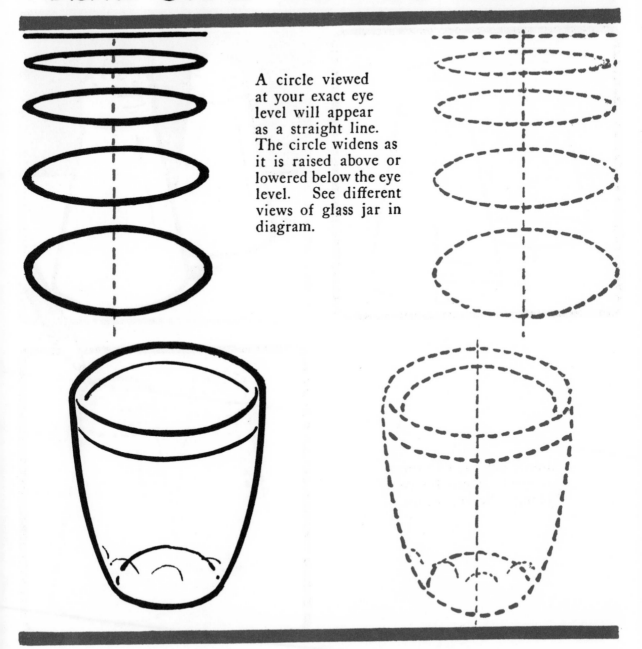

A circle viewed at your exact eye level will appear as a straight line. The circle widens as it is raised above or lowered below the eye level. See different views of glass jar in diagram.

DRAW SIMPLE THINGS!

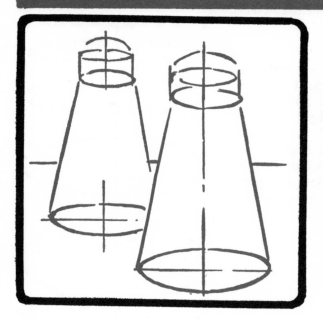

Simple objects, like these,
are good subjects for your
'Things I See' drawings.

YOUR CAP and YOUR TOP

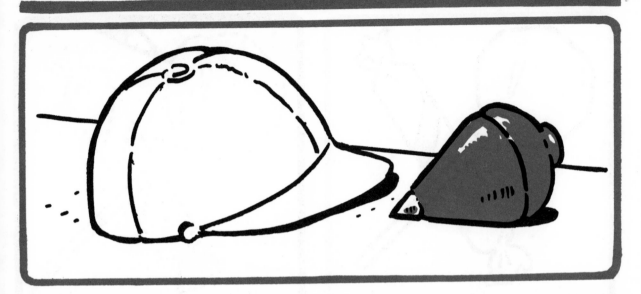

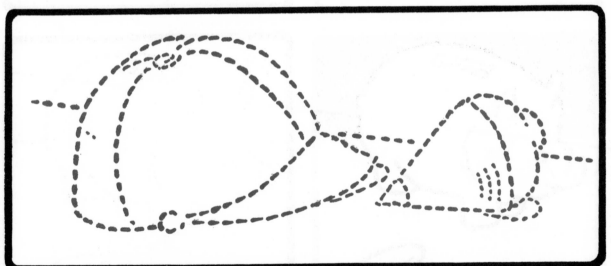

Your cap, top, and many other things you
use and play with, are also good 'models'.

CANDIES and PIGGIE BANK!

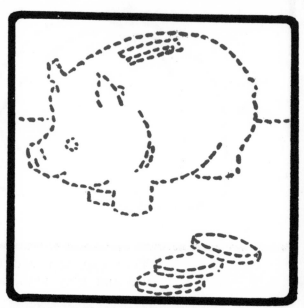

WE DRAW A 'TEDDY·BEAR'

This set of 'step by step' pictures will give you an idea of how to draw your Teddy Bear.

A FUNNY RAG-DOLL!

Here is a good subject to draw. If you do not have a doll like this for a model, just copy these pictures.

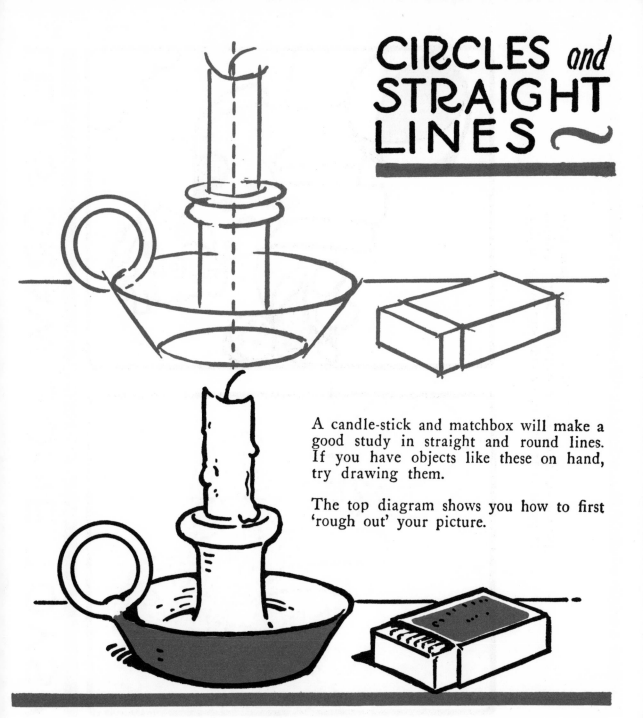

CIRCLES and STRAIGHT LINES ~

A candle-stick and matchbox will make a good study in straight and round lines. If you have objects like these on hand, try drawing them.

The top diagram shows you how to first 'rough out' your picture.

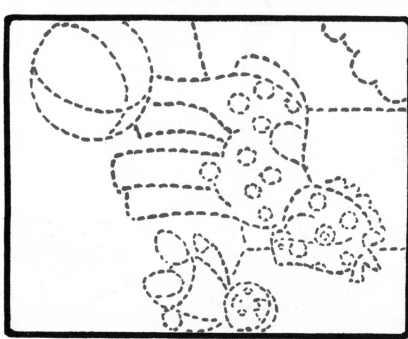

Try to draw this spotted horse. It is an ideal subject. Then practice going over the dotted lines with your black pencil.

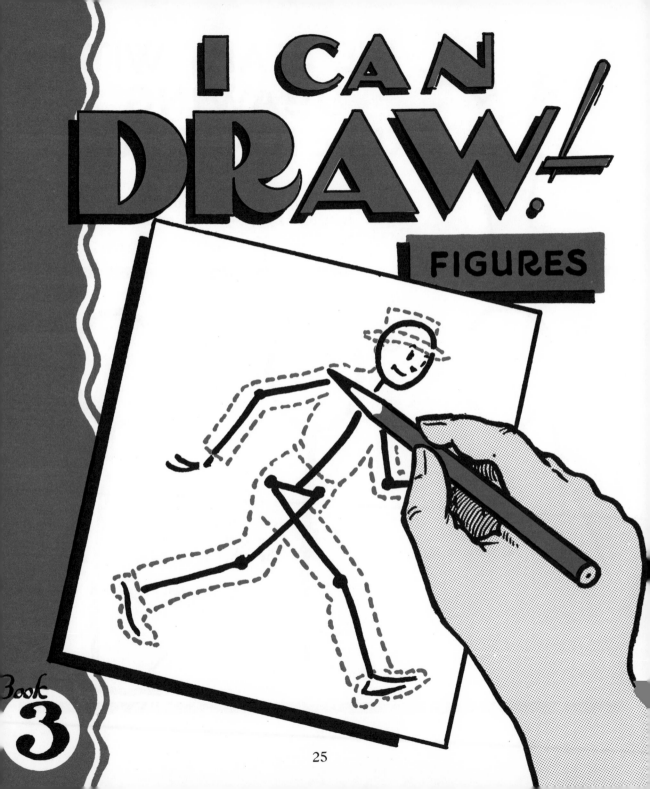

I CAN DRAW!

FIGURES

Book 3

WE START WITH DRAWING "SKELETON" FIGURES!

A skeleton figure is a 'framework' for your figure drawing. Begin with an oval for the head, as in #1.

①

#2-Then, add the long 'body line.' It is nearly three times as long as the head.

②

#3-Draw two lines, each half as long as the 'body line'. One is the shoulders. The other is the hips.

③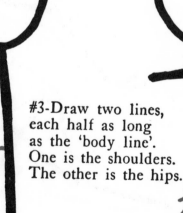

NOW YOUR "SKELETON" LOOKS LIKE THIS

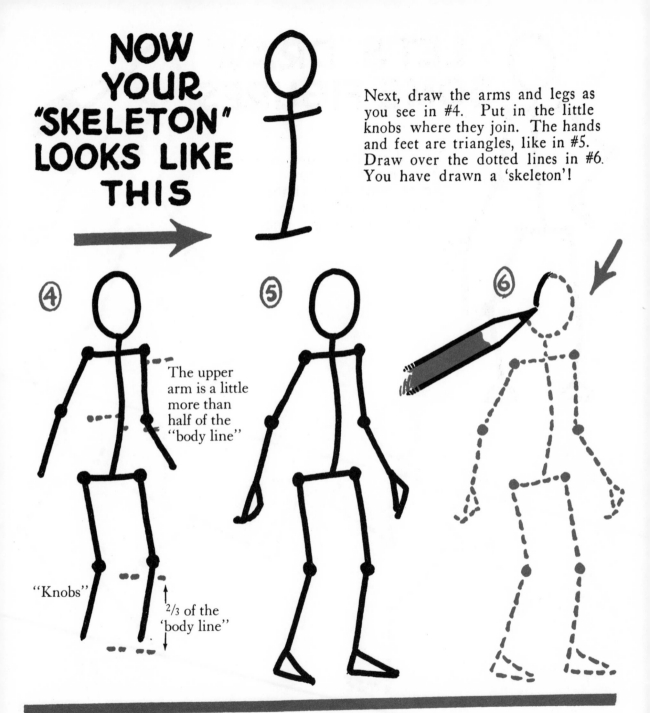

Next, draw the arms and legs as you see in #4. Put in the little knobs where they join. The hands and feet are triangles, like in #5. Draw over the dotted lines in #6. You have drawn a 'skeleton'!

④

The upper arm is a little more than half of the "body line"

"Knobs"

²/₃ of the 'body line'

⑤

⑥

LET'S DRAW SOME FIGURES!

Now draw the figure in action!
Draw many of them.
Never mind their clothes.
First try to get the correct
length of the longer lines.

The FIGURES ARE IN ACTION

Draw many different kinds of action figures.

For good practice exercises draw black lines OVER the dotted figures.

29

THE FIGURE RESTING

Finish these figures with a black pencil. Get the idea of the positions and the length of the 'limbs'.

WE FINISH
THE FIGURE

NOW, if you want to
draw clothes on them,
practice on these.
Go over the color lines
with your black pencil.

The FIGURE WALKS

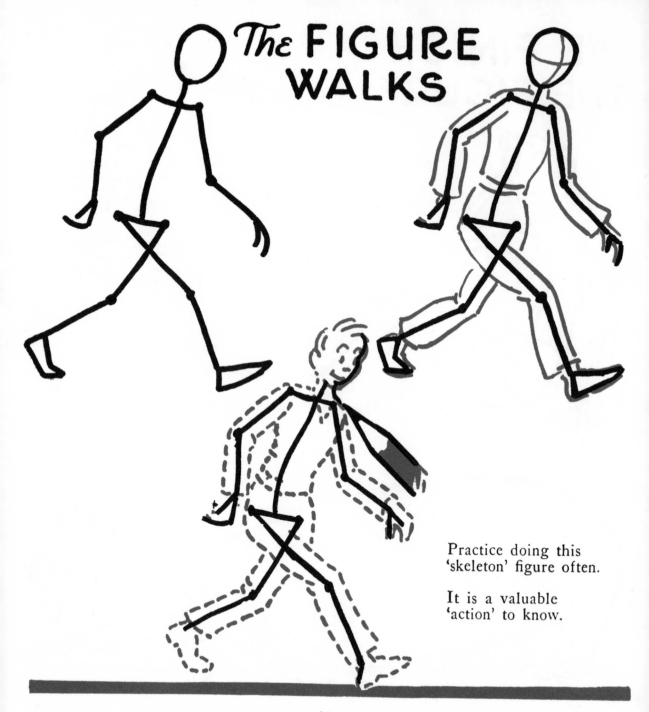

Practice doing this 'skeleton' figure often.

It is a valuable 'action' to know.

The FIGURE RUNS

Do the same with this one, too. Notice that when the arm swings back the foot on the same side is forward.

BOYS PLAY BALL!

First,— draw the 'skeleton'.

Then,— 'block in' like this.

Then finish like this, over the dotted lines.

GIRLS "SKIP" ROPE!

First, draw the 'skeleton',—

and then 'block in'.

The head is drawn this way.

The finished figure is like this.

Here is a good 'action' picture for you to practice on.

Draw carefully over the dotted lines, and then color your picture!

36

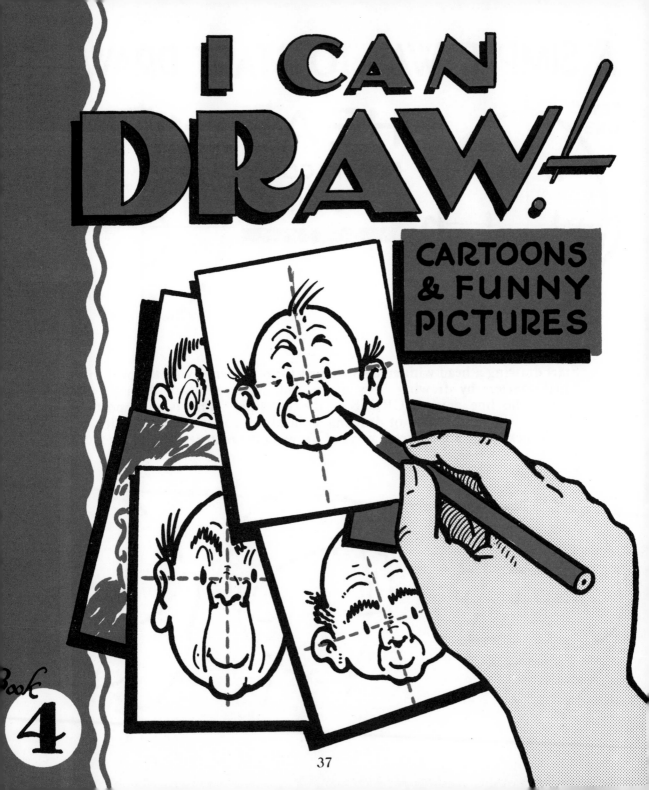

I CAN DRAW!

CARTOONS & FUNNY PICTURES

Book 4

A SIMPLE WAY TO START DRAWING A HEAD

FOR A COMIC PICTURE

"EYE" LINE

Start drawing a head with an oval shaped form. Then divide the oval into equal quarters by drawing lines down and across midway through the oval. The line going ACROSS is the 'eye line'. This is an important line. Below we see ways of drawing a head in partly turned positions. On the next page are different ways of drawing the features on a comic face.

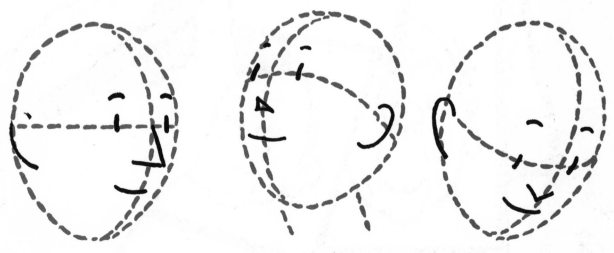

PARTS of A COMIC FACE

THREE KINDS *of* HEADS

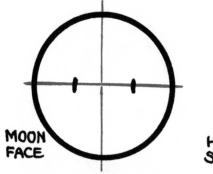

MOON FACE

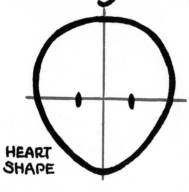

HEART SHAPE

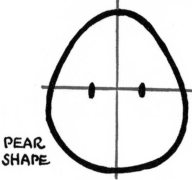

PEAR SHAPE

Here are three different shapes which are used as a basis for drawing comic faces. Below are some of the ways to draw them. Note that by moving the 'eye line' either up or down, you can draw an ENTIRELY DIFFERENT kind of face.

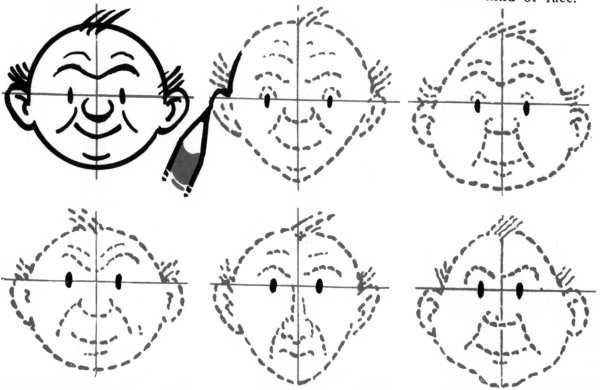

EXPRESSIONS

Carefully draw over the dotted line faces (2) and study the expressions shown on forms (1).

① ② CALM

GLEE

WORRY

ANGER

SURPRISE

FRIGHT

HANDS

Here are some different ways in which hands shown in funny pictures are drawn. Practice by drawing over the dotted lines.

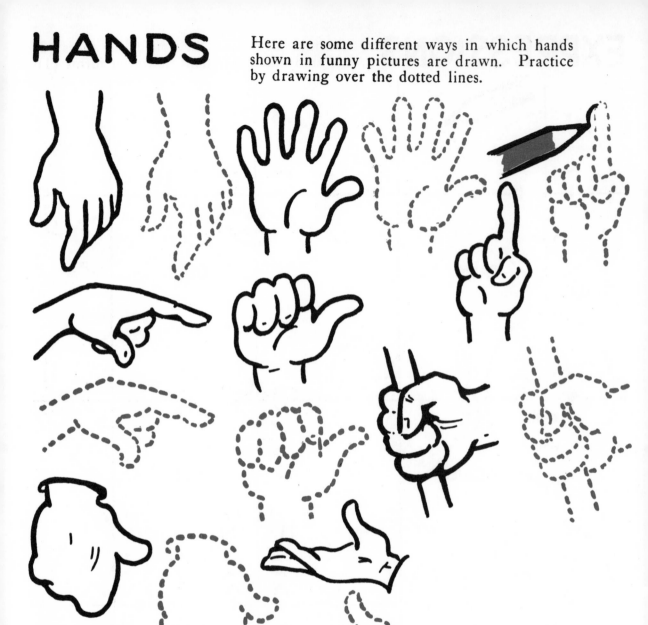

MITTENS FOR
A WINTER PICTURE

FEET

Diagrams 1 and 2 show the easy way to draw a foot. Practice drawing feet by going over the dotted lines with your dark pencil.

SOME "FUNNY PICTURE" KIDS

Start drawing a comic figure by lightly sketching a skeleton form as in (1), then lightly sketch in the head and clothes as in (2) and then finish drawing as in (3).

& "ACTION" IN SIMPLE LINES ~

"FUNNY PICTURE" CLOTHES

Diagrams 1, 2, 3, show three different clothing designs used in funny pictures. Using these three designs, practice finishing the clothes on the outline drawings.

FUNNY FACES *from* FUNNY SHADOWS

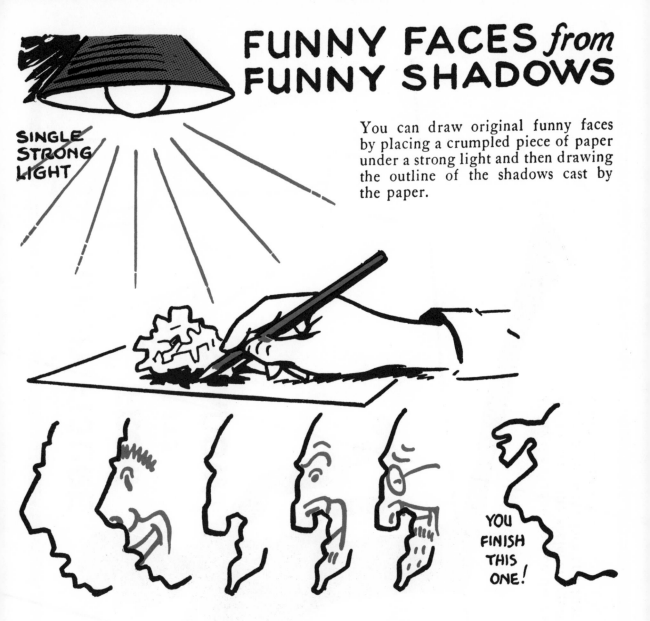

SINGLE STRONG LIGHT

You can draw original funny faces by placing a crumpled piece of paper under a strong light and then drawing the outline of the shadows cast by the paper.

YOU FINISH THIS ONE!

Here are several faces drawn from outlines made in the above manner.

A FUNNY FIGURE FROM ITS SHADOW!

Using the shadow cast on the wall as a guide, try to finish the skeleton figure by drawing the proper funny face and funny clothing to match the shadow.

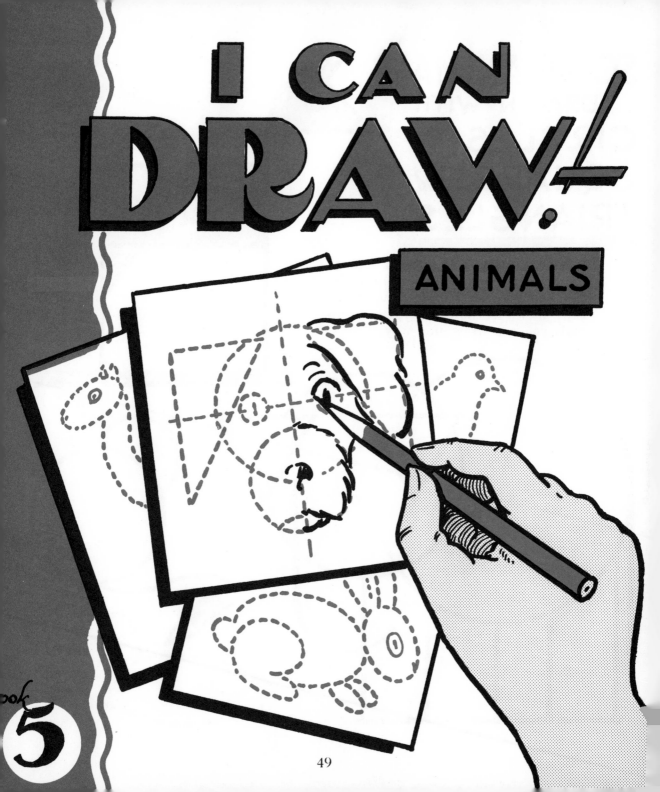

I CAN DRAW!

ANIMALS

book 5

SOME ANIMALS
DRAWN WITH
CIRCLES
SQUARES and
TRIANGLES

Here are a few examples of how to draw animal pictures, using only circles, squares and triangles After you copy these, see how many other animals you can draw this way

LET'S DRAW OUR DOG-!

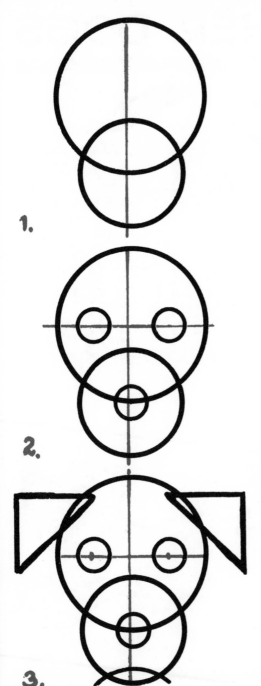

1.

2.

3.

It is easy to draw a dog's head if you follow these simple instructions. Make a large circle with your compass, and then draw a vertical diameter line. Using the base of your diameter line as the center, and with your compass, draw a smaller circle to intersect the larger one. Now insert very small circles for the eyes and the nose. Draw a pair of triangles for the ears, and a curved line for the mouth. Now draw over the dotted lines with your dark pencil.

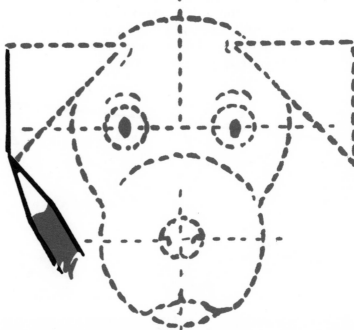

-and SOME OTHER DOGS

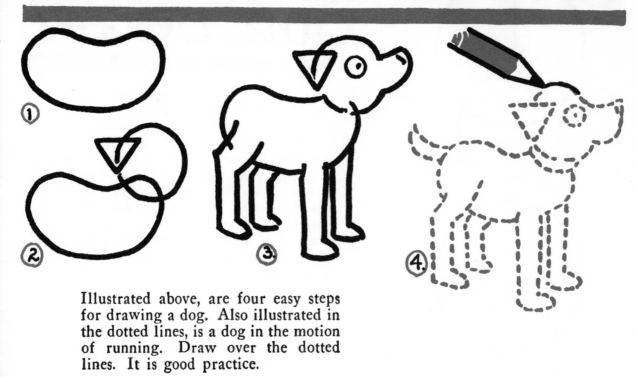

Illustrated above, are four easy steps for drawing a dog. Also illustrated in the dotted lines, is a dog in the motion of running. Draw over the dotted lines. It is good practice.

A CAT IS LIKE THIS

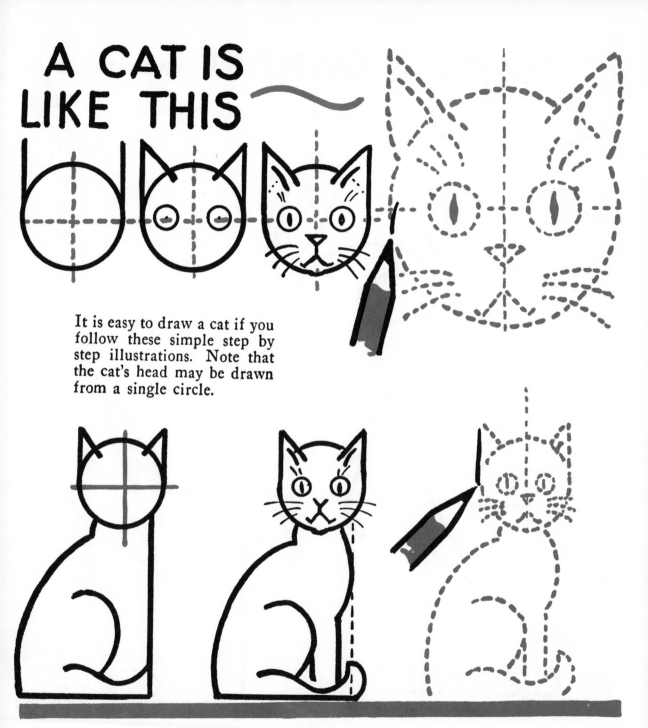

It is easy to draw a cat if you follow these simple step by step illustrations. Note that the cat's head may be drawn from a single circle.

A RABBIT

Here are some more step by step illustrations.

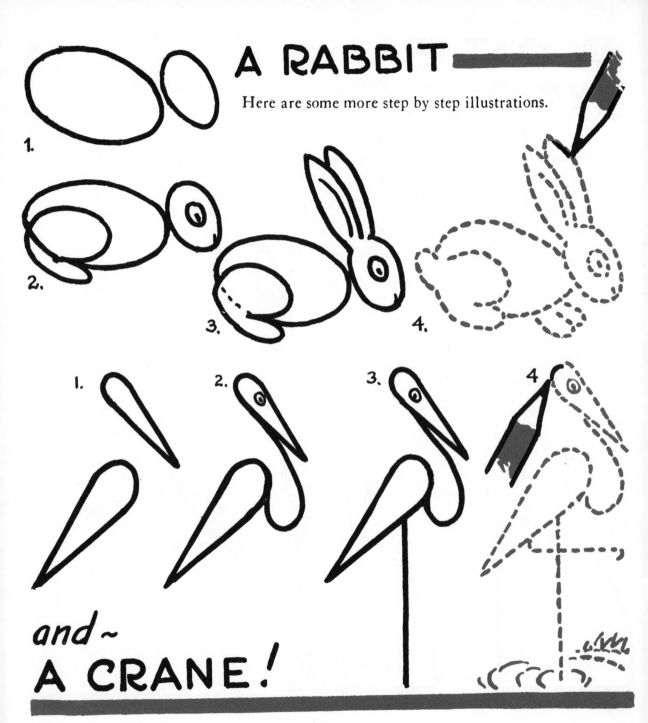

and~
A CRANE!

54

A GOAT and — A SQUIRREL

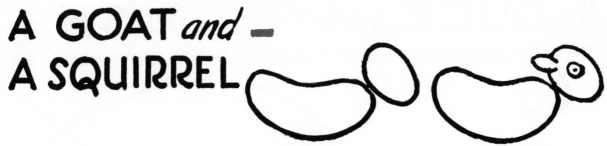

Some more simple step by step drawings.

1.

2.

3.

4.

5.

1.

2.

3.

4.

A DUCK and A FISH ~

A CAMEL
on the DESERT

To draw a camel, first draw a small egg shaped ellipse and a larger egg shaped ellipse. Be sure you allow sufficient room between them to draw in the curved neck. Then add two small triangles on his back to represent the humps, draw his long legs, and you have a camel. Now practice going over the dotted lines with your dark pencil.

WE DRAW A HORSE

By plotting a graph over any picture, you can learn to draw any animal merely by carefully copying the content of each square that has any lines in it.

58

·AND NOW A COW!

Do the same with this picture of a cow, making the squares as large as desired. Then draw over the dotted line picture with your dark pencil.

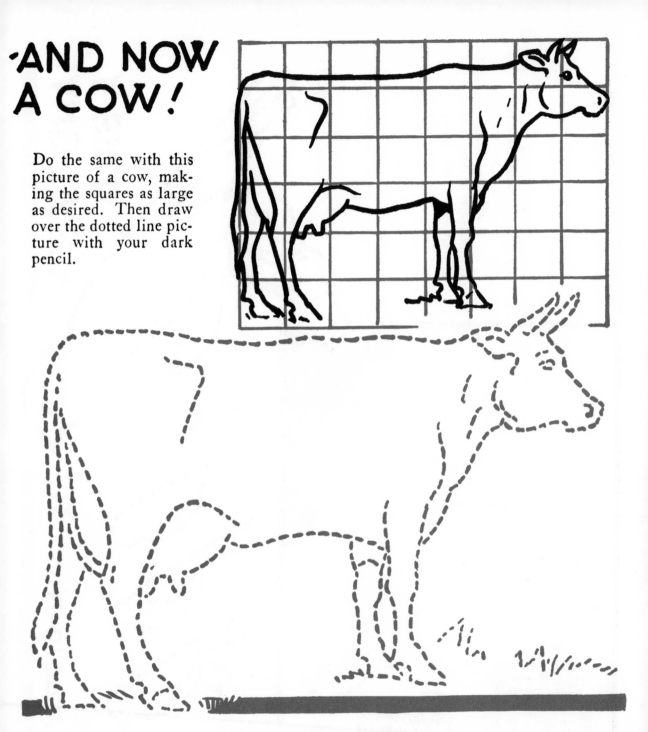

59

AND LAST— A BIRD!

"STEP-BY-STEP"

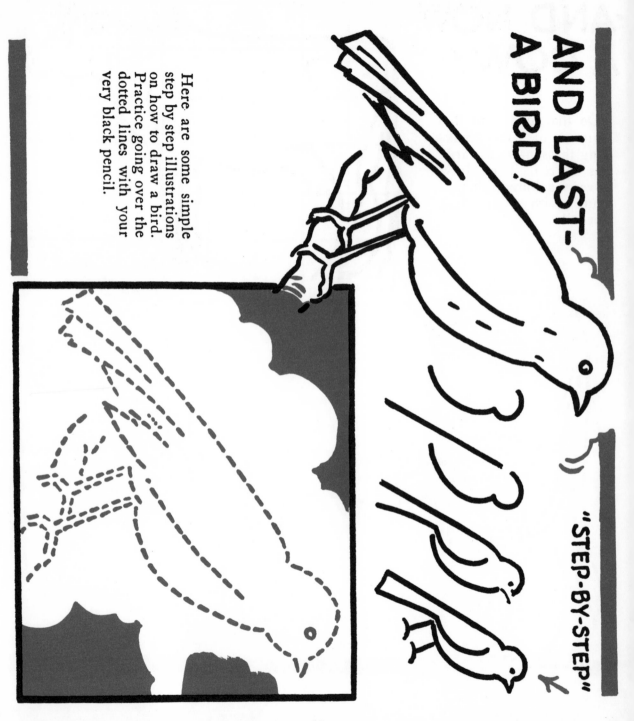

Here are some simple step by step illustrations on how to draw a bird. Practice going over the dotted lines with your very black pencil.

I CAN DRAW!

SCENES

YOUR "SCENE" PICTURE CAN BE MADE UP OF SEVERAL THINGS

Study these pictures of a barn, a tree and a stone fence. Then draw over the dotted lines with your black pencil.

NOW,~YOU ARRANGE IT

Here is a picture scene formed by grouping together the tree, barn and stone fence. Now try to arrange different scenes in each of the other four panels.

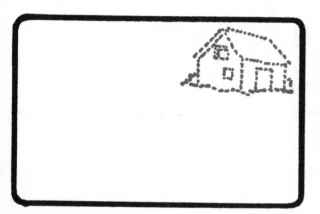

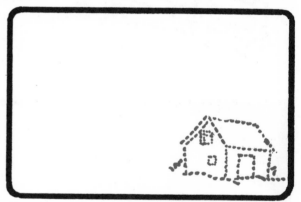

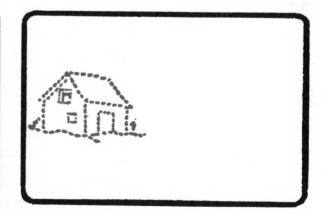

A SCENE TO DRAW

Finish this picture by filling in the details around these three outlines. Then draw over the dotted lines in the rearranged picture below, and finish that scene.

PARTS OF A SCENE

Try to combine one or more of these sketches with your own ideas and draw some original scenes.

THE HORIZON LINE

Here are scenes where we show a LINE where the earth and sky seem to meet. This is called the horizon line. Draw over the dotted lines and finish the water scene.

HIGH and LOW HORIZONS

The horizon line is ALWAYS on level with the eye of the one who views it. In a picture it can be placed high or low. Notice in #3 how the lines of the road meet when they reach the horizon line. That point is called the VANISHING POINT.

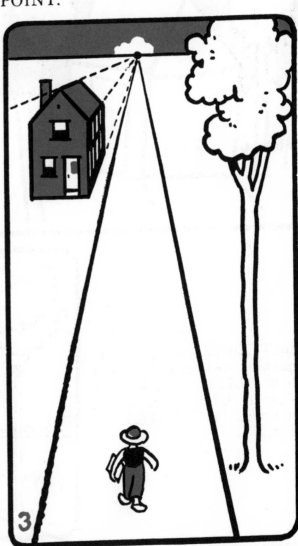

PERSPECTIVE *and-*

In this picture NO use of perspective has been made.

In THIS picture perspective has been used correctly. Notice how ALL the parallel lines slant to ONE point on the horizon, the VANISHING POINT.

VANISHING POINTS

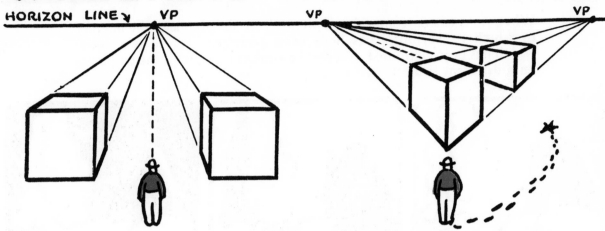

Sometimes, there are TWO VANISHING POINTS in a picture depending upon where the viewing point is located. See how the vanishing point in the first illustration develops into TWO VANISHING POINTS when the man moves to a different viewing point.

"COMPOSING" A PICTURE

When we speak of 'composing a picture', we simply mean the manner in which its various parts have been arranged. Here is a scene which has been composed in several different ways, with the emphasis on a different subject each time.

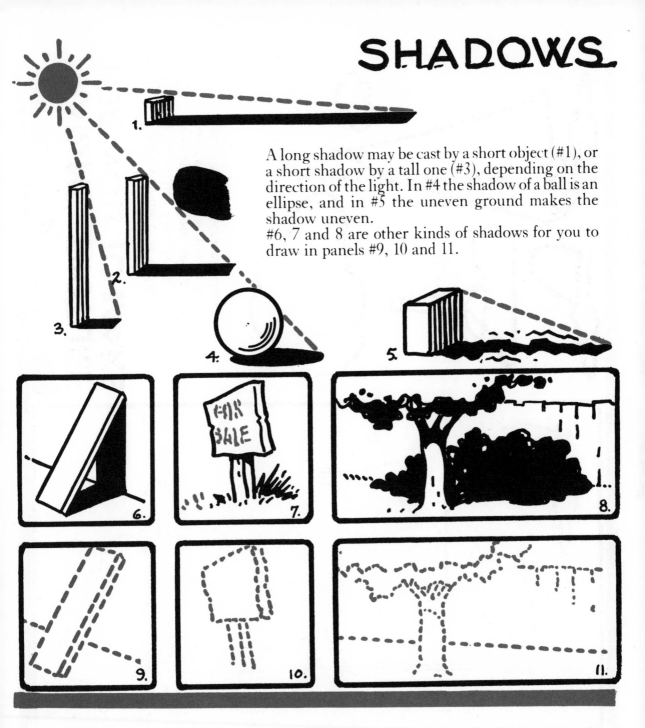

SHADOWS

1.

A long shadow may be cast by a short object (#1), or a short shadow by a tall one (#3), depending on the direction of the light. In #4 the shadow of a ball is an ellipse, and in #5 the uneven ground makes the shadow uneven.

#6, 7 and 8 are other kinds of shadows for you to draw in panels #9, 10 and 11.

2.

3.

4.

5.

6.

7.

SALE

8.

9.

10.

11.

A MARINE PICTURE FOR YOU TO MAKE

First finish the dotted line picture at the right. Then try to compose your own picture, using all or as many subjects as possible that appear in the picture below.

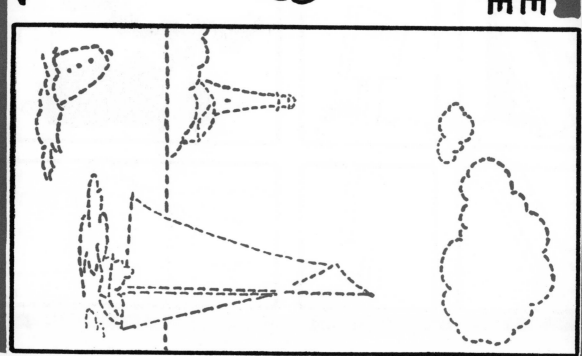

72

I CAN DRAW!

TREES FLOWERS and FRUIT

Book 7

AN EASY WAY TO DRAW A TREE

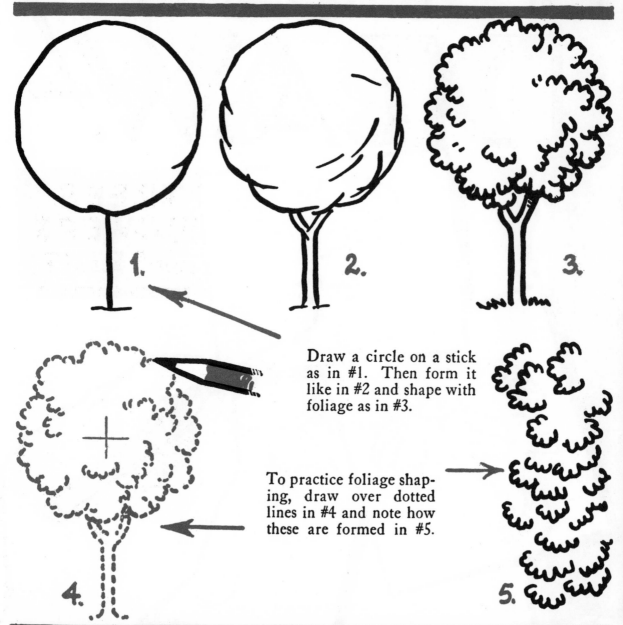

Draw a circle on a stick as in #1. Then form it like in #2 and shape with foliage as in #3.

To practice foliage shaping, draw over dotted lines in #4 and note how these are formed in #5.

MORE CIRCLES ~ BIGGER TREES

To draw larger trees, use three or more circles and follow the same procedure to form and shape tree with foliage.

TREES OF OTHER FORMS~

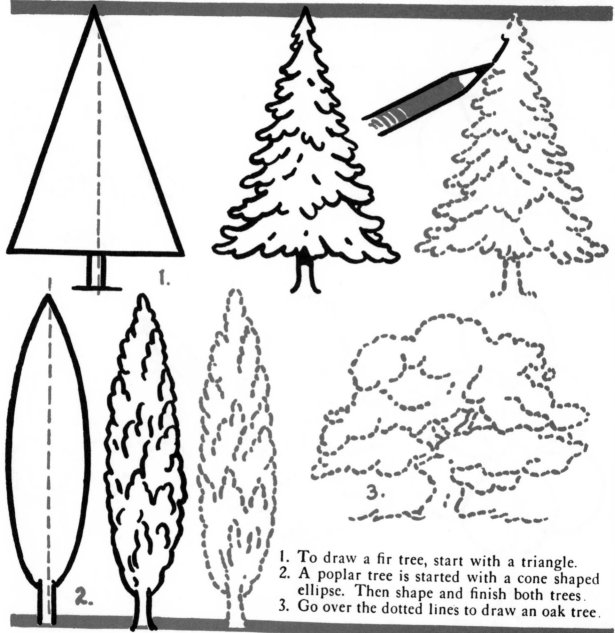

1. To draw a fir tree, start with a triangle.
2. A poplar tree is started with a cone shaped ellipse. Then shape and finish both trees.
3. Go over the dotted lines to draw an oak tree.

A TREE IN WINTER AND SUMMER:

The top two drawings illustrate a tree, barren in winter and in full summer bloom. Draw over the dotted line drawings for good practice.

THREE KINDS OF LEAVES TO DRAW

Most of us are familiar with the elm, maple and oak leaves. Learn how to draw them, by going over the dotted line leaves.

DRAW LEAVES and FLOWERS!

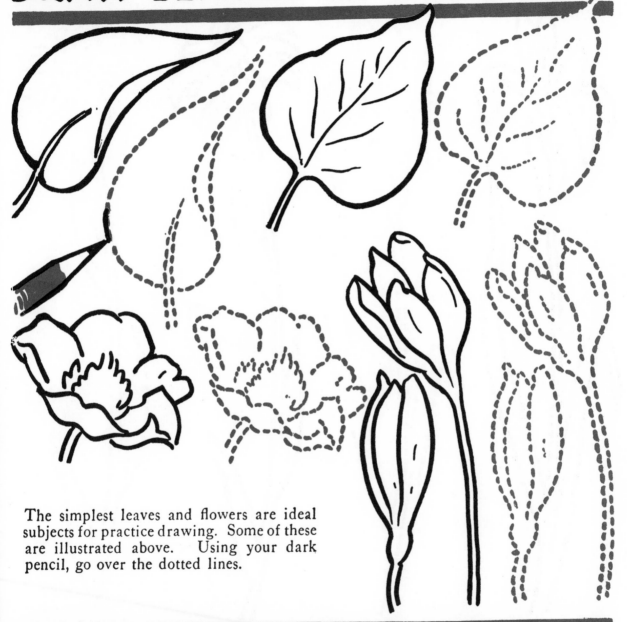

The simplest leaves and flowers are ideal subjects for practice drawing. Some of these are illustrated above. Using your dark pencil, go over the dotted lines.

LET'S DRAW MORE FLOWERS!

APPLES AND PEARS

Apples and pears are always good subjects for picture drawing.

81

NOW WE DRAW MORE FRUIT!

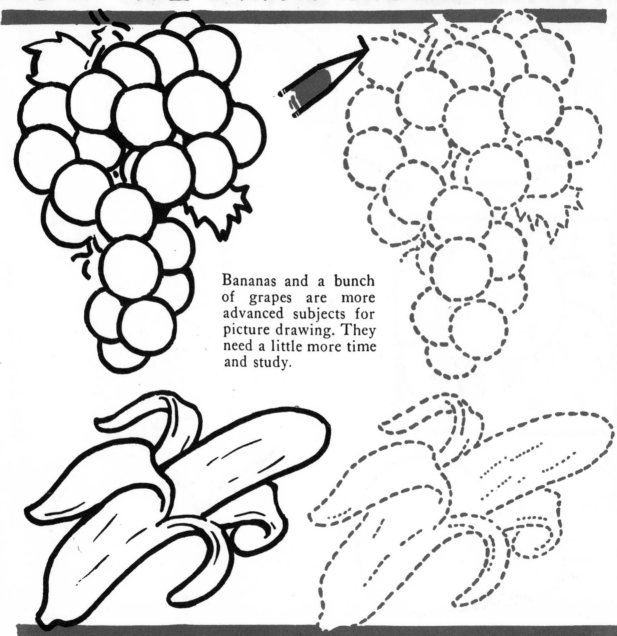

Bananas and a bunch of grapes are more advanced subjects for picture drawing. They need a little more time and study.

MAKE "DESIGNS" FROM FLOWER PICTURES

First, draw a line down the center of your paper.

Then fold the paper EXACTLY on the line.

Draw a part of a flower on one side only of the center line.

Place on a smooth hard surface.

Place another piece of paper over it, hold firmly in place, and rub with a hard pointed object or HARD LEAD PENCIL.

Then open the folded sheet, and observe the completed design.

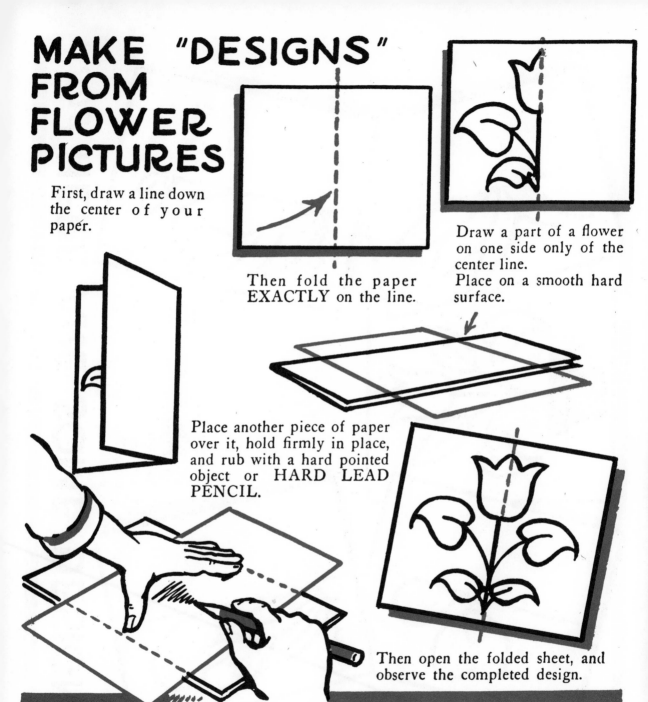

Here are some suggested designs. Try to draw them and see what results you can obtain, following the instructions on page 83. Then try some of your own ideas and designs.

I CAN DRAW!

and MAKE A REAL PICTURE!

Book 8

WHEN SKETCHING OUTDOORS

Cut an opening in the center of a piece of cardboard and then hold it until you have framed in the center of the opening what you consider to be the most appealing part of any outdoor scene. The lower sketch shows how you can omit any uninteresting parts of a scene.

or DRAWING SIMPLE SCENES

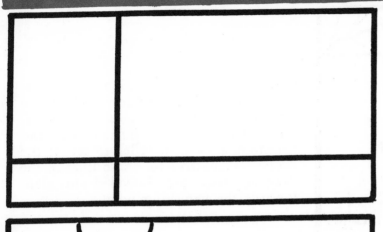

A vertical and horizontal line intersecting each other like in the top panel, can be made the basis of a simple scene.

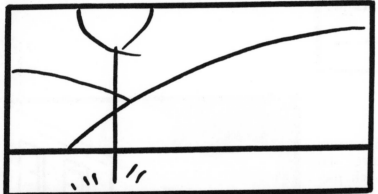

Then draw a long and short line across the vertical line, two rounded strokes at the top and a few strokes at the bottom of the vertical line, like in the center panel.

Now proceed to shape and form the picture by adding the finishing lines and touches, like in the bottom panel.

MORE ABOUT PERSPECTIVE

Oftentimes, the horizon line and vanishing points will be hidden, like in the top picture. In such cases, it is necessary to draw imaginary horizon lines and vanishing points, in order to secure the proper perspective for those lines in the drawing that are intended to slant towards the vanishing point.

The vanishing point is located outside the limits of the bottom picture. To secure proper perspectives in such pictures, make certain you first locate the imaginary vanishing point before proceeding with the drawing.

A CIRCLE IN PERSPECTIVE

If you hold up a cardboard circle like this, it will LOOK like a true circle.

But when you view it lying on a table, it seems to be in the shape of an ellipse.

THREE VIEWS OF A BASKET

SHOWING CIRCLES "IN PERSPECTIVE"

DRAW THE "CIRCLES"!

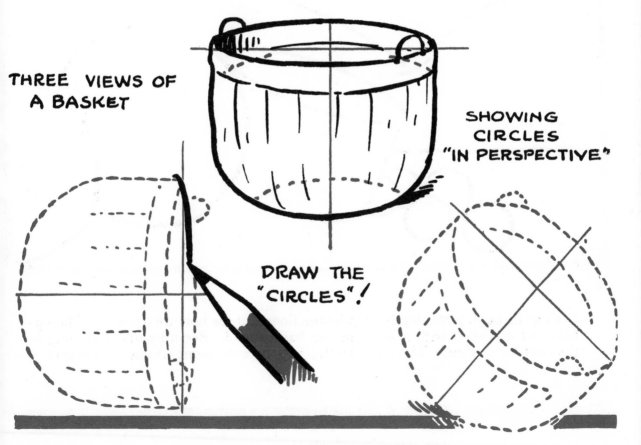

THE BEGINNING of a PICTURE

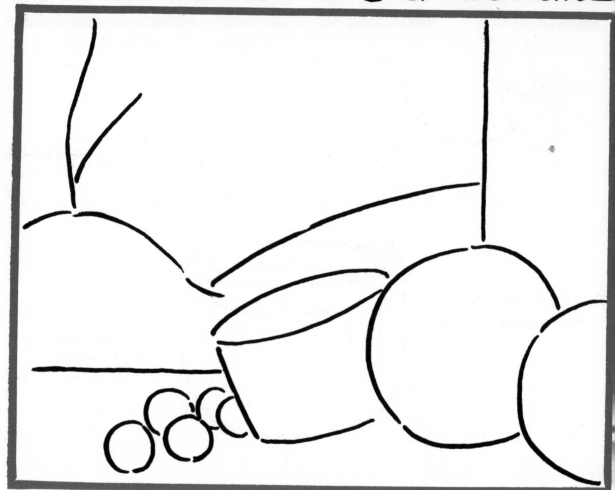

Let's go through some step by step instructions and see how we draw some pumpkins and a basket, with a scene in the background. Begin by first sketching in the simplest outlines. The large circles will become pumpkins as we progress.

Now we begin to add a little form and shape to the pumpkin and basket by adding a few lines here and there. Then we start the lines of an ear of corn hanging on the wall. Draw a few lines to represent a fence and a few more curving lines for some trees in the background.

BACKGROUND *and* DISTANCE

Continue to add some more finishing lines to the basket and the pumpkins. We begin to see the shape of things to come. Proceed to draw the fence by adding some short horizontal lines. Then a few more curving strokes added to the trees in the background will improve their form and shape.

~ SOME MORE DETAILS

Observe the importance of detail by adding some short lines to the corn hanging on the wall. Now we can see some kernels on the corn. The next step is to add some detail to the wall itself by drawing some short strokes here and there. Fill out the drawing by adding some trees behind the fence, and continue to shape and form the different subjects in the scene by adding a few lines or strokes where they will do the most good.

THEN SOME SHADOWS

Add some depth to the scene by using shadows to emphasize and make certain parts of the scene stand out sharply. Darken the trees behind the fence and insert some shadows in front of the fence. Draw the shadows from the pumpkins, the basket and the apples, and make them fall where they will be most effective. Add some detail to the floor boards.

AND NOW IT IS FINISHED!

Add some life to the tree by drawing a few leaves growing from the branches. Now you are ready to add some color to the picture. Fill in a sunset sky, add some color to the basket, the apples and to the wall. Now your picture is finished.

Here is a scene drawn in very simple lines. Copy it slowly and carefully, and then proceed to finish it by using the same step by step method followed in the preceding picture of the pumpkins. If you prefer, draw over the color lines with your black pencil for some practice.

FOR YOUR DRAWINGS

FOR YOUR DRAWINGS

FOR YOUR DRAWINGS

FOR YOUR DRAWINGS

FOR YOUR DRAWINGS

FOR YOUR DRAWINGS